Library of
Davidson College

LOVE BREAKS

LOVE BREAKS

by

OSCAR HAHN

Translation

by

JAMES HOGGARD

LATIN AMERICAN LITERARY REVIEW PRESS
SERIES: DISCOVERIES
PITTSBURGH, PENNSYLVANIA

YVETTE E. MILLER, EDITOR

1991

The Latin American Literary Review Press publishes Latin American creative writing under the series title *Discoveries*, and critical works under the series title *Explorations*.

No part of this book may be reproduced by any means including information storage and retrieval or photocopying except for short excerpts quoted in critical articles, without the written permission of the publisher.

Translation © 1991 Latin American Literary Review Press

Library of Congress Cataloging-in-Publication Data

Hahn, Oscar, 1938-
    [Mal de amor. English]
    Love breaks / by Oscar Hahn: translated by James Hoggard.
    Translation of: Mal de amor.
    ISBN 0-935480-49-8
    1. Love poetry, Chilean. I. Hoggard, James. II. Title.
III. Series.
PQ8097. H26M3513   1991
861--dc20   90-26915
                                                                                            CIP

This project is supported in part by a grant from the Commonwealth of Pennsylvania Council on the Arts.

Originally published as *Mal de Amor* in 1981, then again in 1986, in Santiago, Chile, by Ediciones Ganymedes Leda.

Acknowledgment is made to the following publications where some of these translations first appeared: *Crosscurrents, International Poetry Review, Mundus Artium, New Letters, O.Ars, Puerto del Sol, Sam Houston Literary Review, Texas Observer.*

Love Breaks may be ordered directly from the publisher:

        Latin American Literary Review Press
        2300 Palmer Street, Pittsburgh, PA 15218
        Tel (412) 351-1477 Fax (412) 351-6831

*A mi bella enemiga cuyo nombre
no puede ser escrito aquí
sin escándalo*

*To my beautiful enemy whose name
cannot be written here
without scandal*

TABLE OF CONTENTS

Translator's Preface	9
Aerolito	16
Meteorite	17
Bárbara azul	16
Blue Barbarian	17
Corazón mío	18
My Heart	19
Paisaje ocular	18
Ocular Landscape	19
A mi bella enemiga	18
To My Beautiful Enemy	19
Sociedad de consumo	20
Consumer Society	21
A la una mi fortuna, a las dos tu reloj	22
At One My Fortune, At Two Your Watch	23
Misterio gozoso	22
Joyful Mystery	23
Partitura	24
Musical Score	25
Cuerpo de todas mis sombras	24
Body Of All My Shadows	25
El reposo del guerrero	24
The Warrior's Rest	25
Escrito con tiza	26
Written With Chalk	27
Cena íntima	26
Candlelight Dinner	27
Jugando con fuego	28
Playing With Fire	29
Sobre los hemisferios	28
Over The Hemispheres	29
Ningún lugar está aquí o está ahí	30
Places Are Neither Here Nor There	31
Ecología del espíritu	32
Spirit's Ecology	33
Nacimiento del fantasma	34
Birth Of The Phantom	35

Rocío de los prados	34
Field-Drizzle	35
Fantasma en forma de funda	36
Phantom Shaped Like A Pillowcase	37
Buenas noches hermosa	38
Good Night Dear	39
Con pasión sin compasión	38
With Passion Without Compassion	39
Fantasma en forma de camisa	40
Phantom In The Form Of A Shirt	41
Algo	42
Something	43
El centro del dormitorio	44
The Center Of The Bedroom	45
Sábana de arriba	46
Topsheet	47
Pequeños fantasmas	48
Little Phantoms	49
Cometa	50
Comet	51
Eso sería todo	52
That Will Be All	53
Y ahora qué?	52
And Now What?	53
En la vía pública	54
On The Street	55
Televidente	56
Watching TV	57
Afterword: Oscar Hahn and the Phantoms of Eros	58

PREFACE

When *Mal de amor* was first published in 1981, in Santiago, it seemed that Oscar Hahn had begun using his own experience more directly than in his previous major volume, *Arte de morir* (Buenos Aires, 1977; trans. *The Art of Dying*, 1988), a book that quickly elicited international attention. Characterized by an unrelieved bleakness of tone, one so severe and darkly explosive that it threatened to crush the lyrical impulse, *The Art of Dying* gave powerful voice to what seemed like Hahn's tortured sense of historical estrangement. Ironically, it also showed the obliqueness of his voice. Nightmarish vision was often presented in regular, traditionally framed stanzas that depicted seemingly extra-personal frames of reference.

Then in what at first seemed a more limpid and directly personal mode, Hahn appeared to modify his mythic sense of distance in his subsequent volume, *Mal de amor*, presented here in translation as *Love Breaks*.

The subject matter in the more recent book is erotic, both in terms of the sexual and the more general meaning of the term: the urge for bonding with an Other who simultaneously touches one's mind and flesh. Reading Hahn's sequence of poems, however, we begin to notice the absence of the beloved. There are vivid memories of connection with her, but those memories are often spurred by the speaker's sudden and solitary identification with ordinary objects: bedsheets, towels, dining table, fishbowl, empty parking slots, and rooms that seem forlorn. The speaker keeps being thrown back on himself. His drive toward intimacy is never satisfied. But why? What has caused his sense of loss? In spite of periodically violent airs, there is no intimation of rejection, no image of unrequited love. Again and again, though, we see suggestions, beginning even with the book's dedication, that an important dimension of the relationship is forbidden: "To my beautiful enemy whose name cannot be written here without scandal." In "At One My Fortune, At Two Your Watch," for example, lyrical images of the fantastic turn fractious:

> at three a hotel in flames left
> at four you and I left making love
> at five a man with a pistol left
> at six a shot and you woke up
> . . .
> Now noon strikes
> and I hold in my arms the body of all my crimes

That jagged attitude is even more apparent in "Good Night Dear," where the speaker says:

> May you dream with demons
> and white cockroaches
>
> and may you see eye-sockets
> of death looking at you
> from my eyes in flames

The relationship between the two seems both threatened and threatening, even illicit, and in a heart-breaking way it is.

The speaker is not mindlessly bitter, and the absent woman is neither fickle nor some other man's wife or mistress. But who is she, and what is the meaning of the lovers' estrangement? Throughout his career Hahn has been too poetically careful for us to assume he is simply writing here an open-ended drama whose meaning must be left to conjecture. So we reconsider the work at large. Reflecting on the textures and ideas in the collection, we begin to find answers in metaphors, in analogies, in figures obliquely joining the fragmented world's parts. And the absent woman, we come to see, can be read as Hahn's own lost country, Chile. His pain is the pain of one in exile. Recognizing that, we begin to see how, moving beyond autobiography, these poems fit into the Western tradition. We recall the horror with which the ancient Greeks spoke of homelessness. We notice that morning after morning, despite his wondrous adventures, Odysseus knelt at the edge of the sea and wept for home. We also remember Jacob Bronowski identifying civilization with geographical stability, a centering in place. For counterpoint, we also see, in our own world, images of frenzy and confusion coming from people who find themselves rootless. Their senses deranged, their voices turn shrill and incoherent then fall into pitifully weak murmurs. Everything, including lyrical expression, becomes political; and many voices crack at the strain or, mad to escape the dissembling chaos, lunge for simplistic options before drowning in sentimentality. Some, though, manage to maintain coherence. They are the ones who write what tradition calls the brave songs.

Skepticism and restraint help keep a voice measured and clear, and though he is too open to wonder and grief to be called skeptical, Hahn has indeed chosen restraint to guide the tones of his voice. Ironically, while assuring a sense of aesthetic distance, the tension in restraint keeps alive the energizing possibilities of lyrical expression. We begin to see then that because the world is so splintered, coordination is as necessary as endurance for one to achieve more than meager survival. In *Love Breaks*, as in

Hahn's previous work, personal concerns are transformed into meditative affirmations of mystery. The closure of "Phantom Shaped Like A Pillowcase" provides an example: "her lips began to move / and I heard the clear / crystalline / silence." His suggestive, even allusive, sense of phrasing is also seen in a poem like "Phantom In The Form Of A Shirt" when the speaker turns confession into admonishment: "though you scrape and brush and rub / you can't wash the blood off my side."

Reversals of fortune, though, are facts of life.

One month after *Mal de amor* was first published in Santiago, in the fall of 1981, the government banned it, making it apparently the first book of poems taken hostage by the post-Allende military junta of Gen. Augusto Pinochet. Reportedly no reason was given when books were snatched from libraries and bookstores, and Hahn was not there to protest the rape. He was in the U.S. where he had been studying and teaching. Then five years after the ban, the book was republished in Chile by Ediciones Ganymedes, the same house that had first issued it. The contents of the two editions were the same except for two poems added to the later text: *Partitura* ("Musical Score") and *Televidente* ("Watching TV"). The text here follows the second edition but with Hahn's permission includes three additional poems: "Consumer Society" (*Sociedad de consumo*), "Candlelight Dinner" (*Cena íntima*), and "Playing With Fire" (*Jugando con fuego*).

The love evoked in *Love Breaks/Mal de amor* is not idealized, and the country from which Hahn was estranged is not an abstraction but a portion of earth, an embodiment of spirit demanding justice and wholeness—the fullness of relationship. The book records the serious attention paid to that fact by one who is both insider and outsider. Because of that double perspective and the layered quality of Hahn's language, individual experience becomes associated here with universal concerns. Psychological and physical fragmentations have become commonplace, and terrorism, we come to see, has even turned domestic life political. Intimations of that are clearly seen in the metaphors of romantic crisis described in *Love Breaks*, a crisply wrought collection whose subtleties underscore Hahn's reputation as a major voice of the fantastic.

Nothing comes to stasis. Across the world people continue to disappear, and sometimes only parts of them are found. There are also cries to destroy books, and exhortations and bribes to murder authors. Anger turns hysterical and fear makes one yearn for havens of oblivion. Limbless and headless corpses clot ditches and undergrowth, and across the world printed speech becomes little mounds of ash. Out of weariness, fright, and confusion, potentially elegant voices go mute, but the urge for deep harmony remains; and the force of the will aids that longing. One refuses to surrender. After all, after repeated efforts a mysterious gift of voice may make troubled expression sing, may even make it redemptive.

The misfortune referred to in the title of Hahn's book does not come from adolescent pining but from the nausea that is expressive, Nietzsche reminded us, of powerlessness and estrangement. Refusing the option to yield to the nihilism of despair, Hahn keeps the voice of his poems lively but measured. Without that cautionary sense of control, without that affirmation of continued engagement, gibberish and sentimentality would rise; and when they do, art and morality die.

Although the world has not given Oscar Hahn—and many others of his time—grace and coherence, he has not released himself to the nefarious temptations of fanatical rage. Instead, the idiom of his battle finds its point of reference in that most personal image of unity: erotic love: yin and yang bonding to make the world, bonding to allow individual concerns to become transcendent. In *Love Breaks*, however, that urge remains a longing, the ache that Albert Camus called "nostalgia for order." But we should also remember that that same force is the one that drives us toward coherence of thought, grace of expression, and the mysteries of art.

MAN AS MAP

AEROLITO

La velocidad del amor rompe la barrera de lo real
y el mundo estalla en astillas de sueño
sin la menor consideración para los despiertos

BARBARA AZUL

Aquella dulce muerte tu hermosísimo amor
me ha traído a la orilla de este río nevado
De pronto en pleno invierno la descongelación
descubre rosas rojas y bárbaras azules

Los pájaros helados se entibian sorprendidos
Un trino de color rosado pinta el cielo
a las diez de la noche: y un alba deslumbrante
se levanta a deshora limpiándose las plumas

Aquella dulce muerte tu hermosísimo amor
me ha rozado los ojos con su estela celeste
Y ahora en vez de lágrimas una constelación
de hipocampos dorados rueda por tus mejillas

METEORITE

Love's speed breaks the reality barrier
and the world explodes into dream-splinters
with no regard at all for those awake

BLUE BARBARIAN

That sweet death your most comely love
has led me to this snowy river's bank
Suddenly in the middle of winter, thawing
uncovers red roses and blue barbarians

Dazed, frozen birds start stirring
At ten p.m. a pink trill paints
the sky: and a dazzling untimely dawn
rises cleaning its wings

That sweet death your most comely love
sweeping the sky has grazed my eyes
And now instead of tears golden hippocampi
splash tumbling down your cheeks

CORAZON MIO

Mi corazón bajo la forma de un óvulo palpitante
eyacula millares de corazones diminutos
se embaraza a sí mismo y se da a luz
adentro de tu pecho estás más loco
me decías mirándome fijamente a los ojos
Y el malhadado corazón
a punto de salírsenos por la boca

PAISAJE OCULAR

Si tus miradas
salen a vagar por las noches
las mariposas negras huyen despavoridas
tales son los terrores
que tu belleza disemina en sus alas

A MI BELLA ENEMIGA

No seas vanidosa amor mío
porque para serte franco
tu belleza no es del otro mundo
Pero tampoco es de éste

MY HEART

Shaped like a throbbing ovule my heart
ejaculates thousands of tiny hearts
is impregnated by itself and is born
within your breast you are delirious
you told me looking me straight in the eye
And the wretched heart
ready to burst out our mouths

OCULAR LANDSCAPE

If your glances
go wandering out through the nights
black butterflies flee terrified
so great are the terrors
your beauty spreads in their wings

TO MY BEAUTIFUL ENEMY

Don't be vain my love
because to be blunt
your beauty is not from the other world
But it's not from this one either

SOCIEDAD DE CONSUMO

Caminamos de la mano por el supermercado
entre las filas de cereales y detergentes

Avanzamos de estante en estante
hasta llegar a los tarros de conserva

Examinamos el nuevo producto
anunciado por la televisión

Y de pronto nos miramos a los ojos
y nos sumimos el uno en el otro

y nos consumimos

CONSUMER SOCIETY

Holding hands we walk through the supermarket
down aisles of cereals and detergents

We follow the shelves
to the canned goods

We examine the new product
advertised on TV

Suddenly we look at each other
and dive into each other's eyes

and devour each other

A LA UNA MI FORTUNA, A LAS DOS TU RELOJ

Estuve toda la noche parado frente a tu puerta
esperando que salieran tus sueños

A la una salió una galería de espejos
a las dos salió una alcoba llena de agua
a las tres salió un hotel en llamas
a las cuatro salimos tú y yo haciendo el amor
a las cinco salió un hombre con una pistola
a las seis se oyó un disparo y despertaste

A las siete saliste apurada de tu casa
a las ocho nos encontramos en el Hotel Valdivia
a las nueve nos multiplicamos en los espejos
a las diez nos tendimos en la cama de agua
a las once hicimos el amor hasta el exterminio

Ahora son las doce del día
y tengo entre mis brazos al cuerpo de todos mis delitos

MISTERIO GOZOSO

Pongo la punta de mi lengua golosa en el centro mismo
del misterio gozoso que ocultas entre tus piernas
tostadas por un sol calientísimo el muy cabrón ayúdame
a ser mejor amor mío limpia mis lacras libérame de todas
mis culpas y arrásame de nuevo con puros pecados
   originales, ya?

AT ONE MY FORTUNE,
AT TWO YOUR WATCH

I stood all night facing your door
waiting for your dreams to leave

At one a gallery of mirrors left
at two a water-filled alcove left
at three a hotel in flames left
at four you and I left making love
at five a man with a pistol left
at six a shot and you woke up

At seven worried you left your house
at eight we met in the Hotel Valdivia
at nine we were multiplied in mirrors
at ten we stretched out on the waterbed
at eleven we blew our minds out loving

Now noon strikes
and I hold in my arms the body of all my crimes

JOYFUL MYSTERY

I place the tip of my honey-hungry tongue in the exact
    center
of the joyful mystery you hide between your legs
toasted by a blazing-hot sun the old bastard help me
to be better my love wipe my tears free me from all
my guilts and raze me again with pure original sins, right?

PARTITURA

La música de las esferas
no la produce la rotación
de los planetas en el cielo
    sino la frotación
de los cuerpos en la tierra

CUERPO DE TODAS MIS SOMBRAS

Arbol de todos mis soles
sol de todas mis sangres
sangre de todas mis heridas
herida de todas mis muertes

EL REPOSO DEL GUERRERO

Caballos blancos
    en la mar celeste
que no videntes
    van volando a tientas
pasan rozando
    las espumas lentas
movidos
    por el viento
        del Oeste

MUSICAL SCORE

The music of the spheres
isn't made by planets
spinning in the sky
      but by bodies
rubbing together on earth

BODY OF ALL MY SHADOWS

Tree of all my suns
sun of all my bloods
blood of all my wounds
wound of all my deaths

THE WARRIOR'S REST

White horses
      hovering hesitantly
blindly
      on the skyblue sea
barely brushing
      the slow waves
blown
      by the wind
           from the West

ESCRITO CON TIZA

Uno le dice a Cero que la nada existe
Cero replica que Uno tampoco existe
porque el amor nos da la misma naturaleza

Cero más Uno somos Dos le dice
y se van por el pizarrón tomados de la mano

Dos se besan debajo de los pupitres
Dos son Uno cerca del borrador agazapado
y Uno es Cero mi vida

Detrás de todo gran amor la nada acecha

CENA INTIMA

Miro por la ventana en la noche
Miro el estacionamiento del edificio

Veo dos luces que entran
y se detienen junto a mi auto

Prendo con cuidado las velas
y pongo tu canción favorita

Pero nadie golpea la puerta
nadie golpea la puerta
nadie golpea la puerta

WRITTEN WITH CHALK

One tells Zero: Nothing exists
Zero replies: One doesn't either
because love makes us alike

Zero plus One we are Two he says
and hand in hand they go through the blackboard

Two kiss under the desks
Two are One near the hidden eraser
and One is Zero my life

Behind all great love nothingness skulks

CANDLELIGHT DINNER

I look at the night through the window
I look at the building's parking slots

I see two lights approaching
and they stop beside my car

Anxious I light the candles
and put on your favorite song

But no one knocks at the door
no one knocks at the door
no one knocks at the door

JUGANDO CON FUEGO

Cada sombra en mi ventana
cada ruido cerca de mi puerta
hacen saltar mi corazón

Ahora te toca a ti amor mío

Que esta sombra sea tu sombra
que estos ruidos sean tus pasos
acercándose a mi puerta

antes que la sombra en tu ventana
y los ruidos que escuchas
hagan saltar tu corazón

y nadie llegue a tu puerta

SOBRE LOS HEMISFERIOS

Tú sueñas conmigo en el hemisferio sur
y mi cama proyecta dos sombras

Yo sueño contigo en el hemisferio norte
y cruje el piso de tu dormitorio

Nuestros cuerpos caminan tomados de la mano
sobre los hemisferios

PLAYING WITH FIRE

Each shadow on my window
each noise near my door
makes my heart jump

Now it's your turn my love

May this shadow be your shadow
these noises your steps
coming up to my door

before the shadow in your window
and the noises you listen to
make your heart jump

and no one comes to your door

OVER THE HEMISPHERES

You dream with me in the southern hemisphere
and my bed projects two shadows

I dream with you in the northern hemisphere
and the floor of your bedroom creaks

Taken by the hand our bodies travel
over the hemispheres

NINGUN LUGAR ESTA AQUI
O ESTA AHI

Ningún lugar está aquí o está ahí
Todo lugar es proyectado desde adentro
Todo lugar es superpuesto en el espacio

Ahora estoy echando un lugar para afuera
estoy tratando de ponerlo encima de ahí
encima del espacio donde no estás
a ver si de tanto hacer fuerza si de tanto hacer fuerza
te apareces ahí sonriente otra vez

Aparécete ahí aparécete sin miedo
y desde afuera avanza hacia aquí
y haz harta fuerza harta fuerza
a ver si yo me aparezco otra vez si aparezco otra vez
si reaparecemos los dos tomados de la mano
en el espacio

       donde coinciden

            todos nuestros lugares

PLACES ARE NEITHER HERE NOR THERE

Places are neither here nor there
Each place is projected from within
Each place is superimposed on space

I am now clearing a place outside
I am trying to lay it over there
on top of the space you're not in
to see if by trying harder and harder
you appear there smiling again

Appear there appear without fear
and move from outside toward here
and try hard try hard
to see if I appear again if I appear again
if taken by the hand we both reappear
in the space

    where all our places

        come together

ECOLOGIA DEL ESPIRITU

Ahora estamos hundiéndonos lentamente en el fango
y lo más raro es que podemos respirar
tóquese fondo ahora tóquese fondo quebradizo
quiébrese el fondo y cáigase al vacío abierto
navéguese un buen rato por el cielo
y húndase en el espacio profundamente en el espacio
y lo más raro es que podemos respirar
tóquese fondo ahora tóquese fondo duro
pálpese el fondo siempre con los pies
golpéese el fondo duro rebótese allí
sálgase impulsado hacia arriba sálgase al vacío abierto
navéguese un buen rato por el cielo
porque ahora estoy hundiéndome cada vez más en el fango
mientras vuelo sin alas por el espacio de la pecera

SPIRIT'S ECOLOGY

Now we are slowly sinking in the mire
and believe it or not we can breathe
touch the bottom now touch the fragile bottom
break the bottom and fall into the endless void
sail fast through the sky
and sink into space deeply into space
and believe it or not we can breathe
touch bottom now touch rock-bottom
feel the bottom always with your feet
hit the hard bottom spring back
sail propelled sail up into the endless void
sail fast through the sky
because I keep sinking each time deeper in the mire
while wingless I fly through the fishbowl's space

NACIMIENTO DEL FANTASMA

Entré en la sala de baño
cubierto con la sábana de arriba

Dibujé tu nombre en el espejo
brumoso por el vapor de la ducha

Salí de la sala de baño
y miré nuestra cama vacía

Entonces sopló un viento terrible
y se volaron las líneas de mis manos
las manos de mi cuerpo
y mi cuerpo entero aún tibio de ti

Ahora soy la sábana ambulante
el fantasma recién nacido
que te busca de dormitorio en dormitorio

ROCIO DE LOS PRADOS

No nos encontraremos tú y yo
no nos
encontraremos ya más
en el solsticio de invier-
no nos
encontraremos nunca más
nunca má-
s s s s s s s s s s s s s s s

BIRTH OF THE PHANTOM

Covered with the topsheet
I went into the bathroom

I drew your name on the mirror
fogged by steam from the shower

Leaving the bathroom
I looked at our empty bed

Then a terrible wind blew
and the lines flew from my hand
the hands from my body
my whole body still warm with you

Now I'm the walking sheet
the new-born phantom looking for you
from bedroom to bedroom

FIELD-DRIZZLE

We shall not meet you and I
we shall not
meet any more
in the winter sol-
stice we'll never meet
any more
never agai-
nnnnnnnnnnnnnn

FANTASMA EN FORMA
DE FUNDA

Anoche fui la funda de tu almohada
para sentir la tibieza de tus mejillas
y decirte despacio en el oído
amor mío amor mío

Mis palabras salieron por tu boca
y regresaron lentamente a mi cuerpo
amor mío amor mío

Tuve pena de mí
y la miré en silencio por última vez

Entonces solos muy solos
sus labios empezaron a moverse
y se oyó puro

                cristalino

                              el silencio

PHANTOM SHAPED LIKE
A PILLOWCASE

Last night I was your pillowcase
feeling your cheeks' warmth
and softly saying in your ear
my love my love

My words went out through your mouth
and slowly returned to my body
my love my love

Pitying myself
I looked at her in silence for the last time

Then alone so alone
her lips began to move
and I heard the clear

crystalline

silence

BUENAS NOCHES HERMOSA

Buenas noches hermosa
que sueñes con demonios
con cucarachas blancas

y que veas las cuencas
de la muerte mirándote
con mis ojos en llamas

y que no sea un sueño

CON PASION SIN COMPASION

La destrucción del ser amado por el ser amado
es una práctica común desde la antigüedad

Nos embestimos con pasión sin compasión
y dormimos aferrados a esos cuerpos exánimes

Al amanecer
nuestras cenizas aún lloraban abrazadas

Ahora busco tu amor
en todo resto que pasa por mi puerta

GOOD NIGHT DEAR

Good night dear
may you dream with demons
and white cockroaches

and may you see eye-sockets
of death looking at you
from my eyes in flames

and let it not be a dream

WITH PASSION
WITHOUT COMPASSION

The destruction of lover by lover
has always been common

We attack with passion without compassion
and sleep locked to lifeless bodies

At dawn
our ashes still wept embraced

Now I look for your love
in whatever passes by my door

FANTASMA EN FORMA
DE CAMISA

Estuve todo el día entre tu ropa sin lavar
disfrazado de camisa sucia

Te oí llenar la artesa con agua
y abrir la caja de detergente

Te vi de rodillas frente a la artesa
restregando las prendas una a una

Y ahora siento tus manos atónitas
y tus ojos clavados en mí bajo el agua

porque aunque raspas y escobillas y refriegas
no consigues sacar la sangre de mi costado

PHANTOM IN THE FORM
OF A SHIRT

Disguised as a soiled shirt
I spent all day in your dirty clothes

I heard you filling the tub with water
and opening the box of detergent

I saw you kneeling at the tub
scrubbing your clothes one by one

And now I feel your astonished hands
and your eyes fixed on me under the water

because though you scrape and brush and rub
you can't wash the blood off my side

ALGO

Algo
me pena cada noche
y registra mis cajones
en busca de alimentos

Algo
por todas partes
deja imágenes tuyas
a medio roer

Mi memoria tiene miedo
se olvida de sí misma
y desaparece

Algo
sigue masticando
sigue masticando
sigue masticando

SOMETHING

Every night
something haunts me
and rummages through my drawers
looking for food

Half-gnawing
something
leaves images of you
everywhere

In fright
my memory forgets itself
and disappears

Something
keeps chewing
keeps chewing
keeps chewing

EL CENTRO DEL DORMITORIO

Un ojo choca contra las torres del sueño
y se queja por cada uno de sus fragmentos
mientras cae la nieve en las calles de Iowa City
la triste nieve la sucia nieve de hogaño

Algo nos despertó en medio de la noche
quizá un pequeño salto un pequeño murmullo
posiblemente los pasos de una sombra en el césped
algo difícil de precisar pero flotante

Y aquello estaba allí: de pie en el centro del dormitorio
con una vela sobre la cabeza
y la cera rodándole por las mejillas

Ahora me levanto ahora voy al baño ahora tomo agua
ahora me miro en el espejo: y desde el fondo
eso también nos mira
con su cara tan triste con sus ojos llenos de cera
mientras cae la nieve en el centro del dormitorio
la triste nieve la sucia nieve de hogaño

THE CENTER OF THE BEDROOM

An eye smashes against the dream's towers
and complains through all its fragments
while snow falls on Iowa City's streets
the sad snow this year's dirty snow

Something woke us up in the middle of the night
perhaps a twitch a faint murmur
possibly the steps of a shadow on the lawn
something floating but hard to pin down

It was there: standing in the center of the bedroom
with a candle on its head
and wax rolling down its cheeks

Now I get up go now in the bathroom drink water now
look at myself now in the mirror: and from behind me
it also looks at us
with its face so sad with its eyes thick with wax
while snow falls in the center of the bedroom
the sad snow this year's dirty snow

SABANA DE ARRIBA

Me instalé cuidadosamente doblado
entre la ropa blanca del closet

Sacaste las sábanas de tu cama
y me pusiste de sábana de arriba

Te deslizaste debajo de las tapas
y te cubrí centímetro a centímetro

Entonces fuimos barridos por el huracán
y caímos jadeantes en el ojo de la tormenta

Ahora yaces bañada en transpiración
con la vista perdida en el cielo raso
y la sábana de arriba aún enredada entre las piernas

TOPSHEET

I folded myself up carefully
among the linens in the closet

You pulled out your bedsheets
and used me as the topsheet

You slid under the covers
and I covered you bit by bit

Then a hurricane swept us away
and gasping we fell into the storm's eye

Now you lie bathed with sweat
your gaze lost on the ceiling
the topsheet still tangled between your legs

PEQUEÑOS FANTASMAS

Nuestros hijos amor mío
son pequeños fantasmas

Los escucho reírse en el jardín
Los siento jugar en el cuarto vacío

Y si alguien golpea la puerta
corren a esconderse debajo de mi sábana

los pequeños fantasmas

los hijos que nunca tuvimos
y los que nunca tendremos

LITTLE PHANTOMS

Our children my love
are little phantoms

I listen to them laughing in the garden
I hear them playing in the empty room

And if someone knocks at the door
they run to hide under my sheet

the little phantoms

the children we never had
and never will have

COMETA

La herida de mi costado
la herida de mi costado
Quién ha visto la herida de mi costado?

Se fue rodando por el monte abajo
atravesó las calles de la ciudad
y pasó gimiendo frente a tu puerta

Todos los vecinos salieron a verla
todos los mudos querían hablarle
y los niños corrían detrás de ella

La herida de mi costado
la herida de mi costado

Llegó de noche a los confines de la ciudad
y se perdió sin rumor en el horizonte

COMET

The wound in my side
the wound in my side
Who saw the wound in my side?

It tumbled down the mountain
shot across the city's streets
and passed howling by your door

All the neighbors went out to see it
all the mutes wanted to talk to it
and the children ran behind it

The wound in my side
the wound in my side

It hit the city limits at night
and without a murmur disappeared on the horizon

ESO SERIA TODO

Te estoy haciendo un destino aquí mismo
Lo estoy dibujando en las alas de un pájaro
Lo estoy pintando en la pared de mi cuarto

Ahora el pájaro vuela con furia
ahora lanza su grito de guerra
y se dispara contra la pared

Sus plumas están flotando en el espacio
Sus plumas están mojándose en su sangre

Coge una y te escribe este poema

Y AHORA QUE?

Y ahora
qué haremos tú y yo
tomados de esa mano
que termina en un cuerpo
que no es el nuestro?

THAT WILL BE ALL

Even here I'm shaping you a fate
I'm drawing it on a bird's wings
I'm painting it on a wall in my room

The bird flying wildly now
lets loose its war-cry now
and shoots itself against the wall

Its feathers are floating in space
its feathers drenched with blood

Catching one it writes you this poem

AND NOW WHAT?

And now
what will we do you and I
taken by that hand
ending in a body
not our own?

EN LA VIA PUBLICA

Estoy sentado en la puerta de mi casa
esperando que pase el fantasma

En esta mano tengo un recuerdo triste de ti
En esta otra tengo un recuerdo desolado

Y en estas dos que acaban de crecerme
no tengo nada ni siquiera las líneas

Así que estoy sentado en la puerta de mi casa
esperando al fantasma que vendrá a dibujarlas

para que me mueva y me levante y camine
y pase taciturno frente a esa casa

donde estoy sentado esperando

ON THE STREET

I'm sitting in the doorway of my house
waiting for the phantom to come by

In this hand is a sad memory of you
In this other one a desolate memory

And in these two which just grew on me
I hold nothing not even lines

So I sit in the doorway of my house
waiting for the phantom to come draw them

to move me to get me up and walk
and taciturn pass on by that house

where I'm sitting and waiting

TELEVIDENTE

Aquí estoy otra vez de vuelta
en mi cuarto de Iowa City

Tomo a sorbos mi plato de sopa Campbell
frente al televisor apagado

La pantalla refleja la imagen
de la cuchara entrando en mi boca

Y soy el aviso comercial de mí mismo
que anuncia nada
      a nadie

WATCHING TV

I'm back here again
in my Iowa City apartment

In front of the switched off TV
I sip my dish of Campbell's soup

The screen reflects the image
of the spoon entering my mouth

And I'm my own commercial
advertising nothing
                    to no one

OSCAR HAHN AND THE PHANTOMS OF EROS

by Julio Ortega

The poetry of Oscar Hahn occurs at a critical meeting point: forms of the poetic tradition are found in it along with directly experienced voices of daily concern. On the one hand, his poetry in *Mal de amor* acknowledges the distant model of pastoral speech and, obversely, the machinery of the baroque; on the other hand, the watchful emotional quality, the ardent sensibility of these poems, is expressed in an immediate, spare language. This immediacy of speech is certainly a generational characteristic in Hahn, an heir—like Jose Emilio Pacheco and Antonio Cisneros—of similar explorations of the Latin American poets of the 50s: each one an independent poetic configuration, and each one showing a communicative search through common speech. Both lines of influence materialize in this collection which uses technical resources to sharpen the forms of the poems and to capture and transform the materials of urban experience.

Made from various points of connection, Hahn's poetry is a concentrated implosion of formal and colloquial tensions, and that internal tension dictates the form of a hesitant, antidramatic speech apprehended in its own ironic theatre. For Hahn, however, immediate speech assumes the presence itself of the body as crux of the poetic act. Everything in his poetry happens as a result of and in connection with the body, which inhabits the realm of the living and is the gauge of truth. Among the offerings of the poetic tradition, catastrophes of history and the destruction of all order, the body is the space of witness and reference. Threatened, tortured by the "butchers" of power, pursued by ideological and military machines, the body is the center of possible liberation through criticism and humor, but above all through erotic dialogue.

Animated as much by a skeptical vision of the modern world as by a common feeling of festive, popular resonance, this throbbingly physical poetry proclaims its vitality. The poems themselves are living verbal bodies, organic objects that have a unique, non-repeatable existence. Because of that, each poem appears to refer to a complete history; episodic, they confront living things with a certain remote attitude, though without being able to hide the wounded sense of life. Each poem refers to a larger discourse, is an unlikely judgment, a fervent and painful account of the past. Thus for Hahn each poem presents its own technical dilemma and, on the surface, responds with antirhetoric to the rhetorical solutions that the tradition has provided it. Because of that, in a final irony, his love poetry is at times rhetorically "antilove." Made from things implied, allusions, inferences, the poem has a voice beyond its own speech, saying less in order to imply more. Thus the poem is an antiliterary accomplishment in that, in spite of its occasional lyricism, it refuses to be "poetic." It is a specimen in living flesh, whose speech circulates with a vital appetite and passion for the concrete.

It is not paradoxical that a poet who speaks from historical and personal experience has written so little, since Hahn does not write like a witness or a chronicler of experience, but like a poet who has fleshed experience into poetry. The paradigm of experience (lived, refused, lost), the poem assumes, resumes and consumes. Themes, anecdotes, stories and conclusions are the materials that the poem lights up, reveals, and finally devours. The poem is thus made from ardor and ashes: from epiphanous presence and domestic loss, from passion and worry, from flesh and shadow. Eroticism shines in the vicinity of death (Bataille), but also in the domestic comedy of the couple who satiate their dialogue to the point of losing their way and falling apart. The "sickness of love" [*mal de amor*] is that internal contradiction that exalts and tears up the lover; it is also the consciousness of the precarious and impending dissolution; but it is the same vitality of love that passes through the malaise of the language, through the grief of naming the wound of the lost one. That language is delicately dazzled, somnambulant, permutable. "Body Of All My Shadows" [*Cuerpo de todas mis sombras*] names concisely what the body's presence amounts to:

> Tree of all my suns
> sun of all my bloods
> blood of all my wounds
> wound of all my deaths

[*Arbol de todos mis soles / sol de todas mis sangres / sangre de todas mis heridas / herida de todas mis muertes*]

Is he dealing here with the body of the stated subject or that of the woman loved? I believe he's dealing with the subject, which with the fundamental names of his poetic enumerates the realized fullness of the experience; but in the nature of amorous speech, the body can also be that of the loved one, that Other of a multiple dialogue that substitutes names and puts the natural language in crisis. The Other is the center of reference, but it can quickly be transformed into an empty center: the language thus losing its intermixture of roots without restoring the identity of the one speaking. In that extreme, the beloved's absence is the loss of the name:

the Other is a phantom, and the phantoms of eros populate the poet's exasperating vigil. Speaking fades into reductive aphasia.

For that very reason, it is not paradoxical that Oscar Hahn's poetry would speak to us with a full voice, and at the same time with silence. Few poets in Latin America have managed, like Hahn, to make silence speak. The poem is made from speech and muteness. Coming from that cold passage, silence encircles the name; in it the word is more than brief, it's instantaneous. Memory is made from great silences; the poem interrupts that muteness with its naked truth, but it does not escape its cold, lunar and nocturnal edge. Thus it is that we listen to the quiet whisper of that silence that underscores the poem's speech. Between the improbable summing up of speech and the unnamable muteness, the poem is a transition, an attempt at humor and sarcasm but also at anguish and tenderness.

This is a poetry of insomnia, written to conjure up the excessive brilliance of historical horror as much as exasperated solitude. Appropriately, Hahn titled a collection of his poetry *Arte de morir* (1977). The "art of dying," the classical reading of the brilliance of living, is changed in this book into the passion for living in the same uncertainty of these times of unpunished slaughter. From Hitler to Pinochet the extraordinary vulgarity of violence (Arendt) has been made a part of the political systems with the complicity of supposedly democratic powers and institutions.

From Neruda, Hahn retrieves the lesson of "impure poetry" (the modernist notion that the poem can include everything in its subject matter, including discord); from Vallejo, he follows the moral lesson of the absolute necessity of writing (life is more important than poetry, and he only writes what is revealed to him and inspires him, like his own cause, like life itself); from Gonzalo Rojas (the great Latin American heir of the avant-gardists) comes his notion that the poem is another discourse, a speech that is given in the irrepeatable idiom of poetry and in the roughness of language. But Hahn is also a poet whose work has been helped by his frequenting of the Spanish classics (mystic and baroque) as much as popular poetry, from Villon to Nicanor Parra. In spite of his literary sense of family, however, Hahn is a notably solitary poet; he does not belong to any literary group or poetic movement; he is marginal and different. He is probably the most solitary Latin American poet one can find today, though that's not due so much to an aesthetic declaration as to a matter of temperament. Some of his poems are animated by civil and political emotions characteristic of the 60s; others are involved with the ironic vitalism of the 70s; others, in their lucid execution, with paradoxical games of popular humor; others, finally, carry on a dialogue with classical texts, with a nostalgia for pure forms. That internal variety is characteristic of the game of tensions following the circumspect formulation of the poems.

In comparison with other writers, Hahn is also distinct. In his native Chile he was a teacher but not in a university in the capital but at the farthest point away, in Arica, next to Peru. There he sponsored cultural events and was an intellectual of the independent left who supported the socialistic and democratic concerns of Salvador Allende. During the military coup of 1973, he was thrown in prison and feared for his life, and not without reason, given the arbitrariness of the slaughter; luckily, he was set free and was able to leave the country. He lived the frustration of those years of repression in withdrawal, trying to recover from the nightmarish experience of the coup which had destroyed not only the socialistic hopes of his country but which also hovered like a shadow over the individual and social future of the Chileans.

Hahn completed his doctorate at the University of Maryland then accepted a professorial position at the University of Iowa. Perhaps to protect himself from the excesses of reality, he had written his dissertation on the 19th century Spanish-American fantasy short story. Almost ten years after the coup he returned to his country; in recent years he has returned quite frequently. Although, like everyone in exile, he thinks about the possibility of sometime making a definitive return—he lives within two exiles; he's a solitary figure in excellent company (as Alfredo Bryce says so vividly). For several years he came to believe that he would not write any more poetry; in his case that meant that he would only write if he found something truly important to say.

The poetry of Oscar Hahn, happily, proves the existence of the Muses, who after a silence certainly asserted themselves in the poems of *Mal de amor* (1981), thanks to love again, its power and disasters. They are poems that are freer than those in his previous book; they are also leaner and loaded with internal violence and restlessness. Fragments of affectionate conversation that is more mocking than complimentary, they are figures of an allegorical speech that expresses anguish with images that, however, only mask what they lay bare. These poems are animated by erotic ardor and by the drama of the lover, this time worn out by his passion; the fullness of the dialogue, however, is dispelled in the sudden bitterness of the loss. Irony is transformed into an instrument of control, but the subject can only witness to the contradictory vitality of exaltation and worry—that product which Gabriel García Márquez has called "the momentary panic of happiness."

Hahn's better strengths are found in these poems: major concretion waves like a flag; vivid erotic dialogue is woven into the mute solitude of the world, whose parts are a hallucinatory alphabet, a trail of missed significance. Trapped by an absence that clouds it, presence endures the internal wound of its precariousness. And over all there prevails here (disturbed by discoveries and protests, by joys and terrors) the living voice of a poet who is as truthful in his speech as he is in his silence.

Translated by James Hoggard